21 Career
Transformation Tips

by Carl Henry

Cover Design by Brian Halley
Book design by Nichole Ward, Morrison Alley Design

Although the author and publisher have made every effort to ensure the accuracy and completeness of information contained in this book, we assume no responsibility for errors, inaccuracies, omissions, or any inconsistency herein. Any slights of people, places, or organizations are unintentional.

First Printing 2015

ISBN 978-0-9657626-5-6

21 Career Transformation Tips

Contents

	Introduction	i
Chapter 1:	Learn Something New Every Day	1
Chapter 2:	Always Do More Than You're Being Paid For	7
Chapter 3:	Think Outside the Rectangle	11
Chapter 4:	Expand and Exceed Your Own Expectations	15
Chapter 5:	Put in the Time: Work Smarter and Harder	19
Chapter 6:	Know How Your Job Fits into the Bigger Company Picture	23
Chapter 7:	Remember That People Do Things for Their Reasons, Not Yours	29
Chapter 8:	Motivation is Personal and Ongoing	33
Chapter 9:	To Be the Best, Spend Time with the Best	37
Chapter 10:	Someone Else Wants Your Job	43
Chapter 11:	Always Be Interviewing for Your Next Job	47
Chapter 12:	To Master Success, Master Time Management	51
Chapter 13:	Practice Getting Comfortable in Front of a Group	55
Chapter 14:	Pay Attention to Your Personal Brand and Reputation	59
Chapter 15:	Add a Personal Touch to Your Texting	65
Chapter 16:	Make the Right Investments (in Yourself)	69
Chapter 17:	Nurture Your Comic Side	73
Chapter 18:	Take Advantage of Mentorship	75
Chapter 19:	Get Away for a Fresh Perspective	81
Chapter 20:	Become the Expert in Your Field	85
Chapter 21:	Find Your Own Blueprint for Success	91
	Conclusion	95

INTRODUCTION

I've never been a huge fan of video games, but when my son was a teenager he used to play them all the time. One thing that always struck me about the technology today's young people have to work with is that it's so *immersive*. I can remember when video games were about pie-shaped creatures eating pellets and chasing strawberries; now there are entire virtual worlds where tens of thousands of people do battle together.

Of course, because of the complexity involved, there are lots of tricks and tools that the best players use to give themselves an advantage over everyone else. Many of these are learned over time, but some can be gleaned from specialty guidebooks that show you how to beat particular levels, come out ahead in certain situations, or dominate another player.

I learned all of this when, in the midst of a shopping trip, my son asked me to purchase one of these books for him. When I questioned him on why I should do such a thing, he gave a surprisingly well-reasoned argument: "I already have the game, and this will make me better at it." In his own way, he was making an argument based on improved ROI.

"What about the other people who play?" I countered. "Is it fair to them if you know secrets they don't?"

He just shrugged. "I guess if they want to beat me, they should buy the book, too."

The whole interaction was kind of funny, but it underscores a bigger and more important point: In the ongoing game that is your professional career, you are at a severe disadvantage if you don't know the same tips and tricks that the most successful people do. Without that kind of insight, it doesn't matter how hard you work, how many hours you put in, or even who you know... you'll always be falling behind.

For a lot of people, finding true success – that is, not just getting a job and keeping it, but succeeding and reaching their most important goals – remains a hit-and-miss, trial-and-error process. Unless you have a very good mentor and lots of life experience, you're going to take a lot of knocks on the way to the top (wherever that might be for you), and run the risk of having your career stall a long time before you ever reach your potential.

If that sounds like something you can relate to, maybe what you need isn't a more prestigious degree or a better relationship with the boss. Instead, you might just need a simple, time-tested guidebook for success.

That's exactly what I've set out to create, and the result is the text you're holding in your hands (or viewing on your screen) right now. In it, I'm going to share 21 transformational tips with you. If you put them to good use, I promise they can change not only the way you think about your career, but also the results you get as you move forward.

Who Am I to Write This Book?

My name is Carl Henry, and if you aren't familiar with my work, you should know that I spent the first couple of decades of my career as a successful salesperson. From there, I moved into coaching, speaking, and consulting, developing a business with clients in dozens of industries around the world.

And while those facts are all great for me, more to the point is that I've had an interesting relationship with success. I don't mind admitting that I worked my way up from the bottom, with no prestigious education or family connections behind me, and have gotten the chance to partner and collaborate with many smart, driven, and motivated people over the years.

I certainly can't claim that I've made nothing but good decisions, or that I've invented all the concepts that helped me or that you're reading in this book. In fact, my best trait has probably been my curiosity and willingness to learn.

Still, I learned a lot from the hard work that it took me to build up a successful sales career, and then my own business. More importantly, I've gotten the chance to observe top performers in many fields, and to study the way organizations and relationships work from the outside-in as a consultant. The result is that I've gotten a perspective that most people don't – I'm uniquely qualified to cut through the fluff and tell you what you can start doing, today, that will make a difference in your ability to be hired, get promoted, earn more money, and change the course of your career.

Most of what I've picked up along the way seems like common sense in retrospect, but don't feel bad if what you read in the coming chapters hasn't occurred to you before. If being successful were easy, and the advice you needed were obvious, everyone would be fighting for the corner offices. Instead, what usually happens is that a few people figure out what *really* matters at work, and the rest get stuck in their careers without ever really understanding why.

As with all the books, seminars, and workshops I've ever completed, I'm going to do my best to share the important facts and details with you as clearly and succinctly as possible. I can't follow through on it for you, though, so you are going to have to make the decision to change your life. I'll give you the tools, you provide the action.

If that sounds fair to you, let's get started with the 21 tips that can transform your career...

CHAPTER ONE

Learn Something New Every Day

There are probably a hundred different takes on that old adage, and they are all useful for understanding the importance of constant improvement in your career. That's a simple truth, and one that should be easy to understand. If you aren't doing something to make yourself more useful, productive, or knowledgeable, you're at a disadvantage to someone else who is making that effort right now.

In the digital age, coming to that understanding is more important than ever. That's because right now there are more educational resources available to you than at any other point in history. E-books, podcasts, webinars, online courses, and even YouTube clips are all accessible to you – often for a very low cost or nothing at all – if you take the first step of finding them. No matter where you are or what you know right now, you could become an expert in virtually anything in the course of about a year, simply by using the online resources that are all around you.

> **"If you aren't**
> getting better,
> **you're falling behind**
> *someone who is.***"**

There is another side to this opportunity, though, and one that most people don't think about enough: You aren't the only one who has access to that knowledge and those materials. Even if you aren't taking advantage of them, you can bet that someone who is motivated and ambitious will be.

That might not seem like a big deal if you're comparing yourself to your coworkers, many of whom might not be making much of an effort to get ahead. But what about your colleagues in other companies, other cities, or even other countries? Having traveled somewhat extensively over the years, I can tell you that there are bright, driven people around the globe who don't just want to take your job, but to be your boss.

That's not meant to scare or intimidate you, just to wake you up to the reality that there is not really any such thing as "good enough" anymore, if there ever really was. It's up to you to decide how far you want your career to take you, and just what you'll be willing to do and learn to make those dreams come true.

The easiest way to separate yourself from those around you is simply to know more. When you learn something every day, no matter how large or small, you add to your knowledge and versatility. You give yourself skills and insights that no one can take away from you.

It's no coincidence that the most successful people in any field tend to be the ones who cultivate a sense of curiosity. They might be experts in one or two things, but they also have a passing knowledge of broad business subjects like marketing, recruiting, motivation, and productivity. They are always looking for new ways to understand their industries, improve at their jobs, or get more prepared for the next step in their careers.

A lot of people are turned off of the idea of learning, I think, because of the experiences they have in school. But even though I wouldn't dissuade you from increasing your education if you think it will help you, the "learning" I'm referring to in this chapter doesn't necessarily have to entail getting another degree, earning a certificate, or adding a few initials to your business card. Some of the most important learning experiences you can get have nothing to do with classrooms or textbooks.

Consider this: An MBA might help you break into executive circles, but simply learning a few keyboard shortcuts for your spreadsheet, picking up a handful of phrases in another language, or memorizing a few solutions to common customer service interactions might be more helpful to you in your day-to-day working life. Mastering the art of presentations could help you lead meetings and spread your ideas, and reading a few books on psychology could help make you more persuasive. I could go on and on, but the point is that there are a lot of different types of learning, and you should focus your attention on the ones that bring you closer to your short- and long-term career goals (something we'll talk about in just a bit) rather than "checking off a new box" on your résumé.

Saying that you should learn something every day isn't the same as saying you should constantly be studying. You don't have to invest a huge amount of time to pick up new skills and ideas. In fact, the principles of things like time management and business etiquette, for example, can be mastered in a few weeks by devoting 10 or 15 minutes each morning or afternoon.

Being a good learner makes you more productive and valuable. Even better, it opens up your mind to new ways of thinking, so you become versatile and can adapt to new situations. That's a great way to keep expanding your horizons... not to mention stay one step ahead of all the others out there who would like to move ahead of you on the career ladder.

"Your value
to your employer should always be
more than your salary. **"**

CHAPTER TWO

Always Do More Than You're Being Paid For

Y ou've probably heard someone joke, "Let (fill in the blank) take care of it... They don't pay me enough for that!" That kind of thinking is common in a lot of companies and careers. It's also extraordinarily short-sighted.

My advice would be almost the exact opposite: *Always do more than you're being paid for.*

Following that notion will probably require you to put in more time and effort than many of your colleagues, but it's going to be worth it. There are a few reasons why, and not all of them have to do with your employer.

Let's start with your company's or supervisor's perspective, though: When your output exceeds your salary, you are essentially telling the people who pay you that you're a good investment. In a strict dollars-and-cents way, that's a good way to build job security. When an economic downturn comes, who do you think they're more likely to get rid of, an employee who's always contributing something more to the bottom line, or one who seems to punch in and out (literally or figuratively) while doing the bare minimum?

In the bigger scheme of things, doing a little bit of extra work and taking on new responsibilities makes you stand out. Others recognize your effort and might consider you for promotions and new responsibilities. Or you may even be noticed by a competitor who will attempt to get you to join their own company – but with an improved job title and salary. At the very least, it ensures that you'll be able to get positive recommendations from supervisors, clients, and colleagues if you ever do decide to make a change in your career.

Another reason to do more is subtle, but probably the most important of all: Hard work and continuous effort become habitual. The more you get into the habit of working hard, the easier it is to *keep* working hard in the future. That may or may not be a priority in your current position, but you can bet that it's going to become a necessary skill as you move closer and closer to your dreams.

Most of the best jobs in the world are also among the hardest. That's why the men and women at the top are paid the most money, work the longest hours, and take on the biggest responsibilities. They are trusted with tasks and decisions that can't be given to others. That's partly due to what they know, of course, but it also comes down to their own work ethic. If you don't set the right habits now, you're going to have a hard time instilling them within yourself later when it really matters.

Doing more than you are paid for is usually easy. In every business and department I've ever worked with, there were tasks that needed volunteers, skills that could be added, and extra hours that could be put in. Come in just a little earlier and stay just a little bit later. Or look for an area where a little more attention could be paid and then see how you can pitch in. If the solution doesn't seem obvious, ask a supervisor. They won't just point you in the right direction — they'll notice you're someone who has a bit of initiative and potential.

Another way to add value to yourself is by learning new skills. I've already gone into the personal benefits you get from continual learning, but consider things from an employer's point of view: If they hire you while you have one set of skills and talents and you add others while you're on the job (and on your own), then it's like they've gotten a better employee for free. That can be a big deal, especially if the skills you acquire are in high demand.

The wonderful thing about effort is that it's made up of attitude. You can't control your age, your past, or even which talents you were born with. What you *can* affect directly, though – every single day – is the attitude you bring to your work. When you decide to give more of yourself to your job, and your career as a whole, everyone benefits. Learn to do more than you're being paid for and you'll get back so much more in return.

" Creativity
isn't just for artists.
Better thinking always
means better solutions. **"**

CHAPTER THREE

Think Outside the Rectangle

One of the biggest differences between truly successful individuals and all the others who wish they could duplicate their accomplishments is that the best of the best don't see business as a matter of dollars and cents, but a creative challenge. In other words, they think outside the box.

I want you to go even farther and think outside the *rectangle*.

What does that mean? That whatever the accepted rules and conventions are in your business, don't be afraid to challenge them once in a while. Whatever the "box" looks like in your industry, don't be afraid to slide the lines around a bit and see what you find.

Fostering this kind of creativity isn't just important to your career — it's what transforms entire companies. Imagine for a moment that everyone you work with – and all the people you compete against – are using the same advertising methods, pieces of software, and manufacturing systems. The only way to get an edge on anyone would be to do things *slightly* better.

Making small, incremental gains is important to building competitive advantages and squeezing more out of the bottom line, but every organization needs individuals who can go farther if they want to succeed over time. Instead of working with small percentage points here and there, try to envision ways that you can change the game altogether.

There is an easy way to understand this dynamic. Many of you reading this book right now will have bought it, in some version or another, from Amazon.com. At a time when bookstores around the world were looking for new ways to engage readers with displays, or improve their retail stores (in other words, look for small percentage improvements), the founders of Amazon took a different view. *What if,* they wondered, *readers could order books more inexpensively online and have them shipped straight to their homes?* The answers led them to change a whole new industry… and then to change it again with e-books, personalized selections, and subscription-based delivery.

The point here isn't to make you fall in love with Amazon; it's to point out that the decision-makers in the story went outside the usual conventions of their business to think creatively about what might work. You can do the same, on a bigger or smaller scale, to reimagine things like manufacturing, customer service, or supply chain development.

Of course, thinking creatively is easier said than done. So how exactly do we start thinking "outside the rectangle" and get those great insights and inspirations we're looking for?

The easiest way is to simply add to your list of influences. The more you read, listen, and try to understand, the more perspectives you have to draw from. If you are being exposed to new ideas every day, then it's only a matter of time before you'll stumble across one that could apply itself to your job, or the challenges your business or department happens to be facing.

Another way to foster creativity is to actively look for it. Set aside a set amount of time each day (for example, 15 minutes in the morning, when most people feel at their creative best) and just decide to think crazy thoughts. Ask yourself "what if" in a number of different ways: What if you *had* to reduce expenses by 15% this year? What if someone offered you $1 million to find 50 new customers? What if you wanted to be promoted two times in the next three years?

A lot of this brainstorming might come to nothing, but you will be surprised at what sorts of inspirations you can generate over time. What a lot of people don't realize is that creative thinking isn't just about epiphanies that come to you when you least expect them – it's also a habit that you can cultivate. More time spent thinking creatively yields bigger creative thoughts, and more often. Your brain learns patterns, and when it knows you're actively looking for solutions that fall outside your everyday ideas, it will begin supplying them and bringing them to the forefront of your mind.

Sometimes, the best way to improve something is by doing it completely differently. To think creatively, you have to expand your sphere of influences and be willing to come up with a lot of ideas that won't work before you find a few great ones that will. Learn to spot opportunities outside the rectangle, because that's where the best chances to improve your career usually lie.

CHAPTER FOUR

Expand and Exceed Your Own Expectations

I think it's fair to say that most people never come close to realizing their true potential. More often than not, it's because they don't expect more from themselves.

The strongest limits we face in life are the ones we impose upon ourselves. If someone else thinks we're not good enough, we can take comfort in the knowledge that they don't know enough about us, and can't see our inner talents and ambitions. But if *we* decide that we aren't good enough to go any farther than we have, only a random act of chance will move us any farther forward.

For that reason, it's crucial that we expand and exceed our own expectations on a regular basis. We have to keep stretching our own ideas of what we can possibly achieve, and then demand more from ourselves.

One straightforward way to do this is by setting short-term targets that are ambitious but reasonable. When thinking of what you can do in your life and career in the

" **It doesn't matter**
what others think
You'll always get
exactly what you expect from yourself. "

next few months, for example, you can look to improve yourself in a few key ways. Doing that moves you forward at a sustainable pace, but it also gives you a taste of success and allows you to think bigger.

I'll give you an example from my work as a sales trainer and coach. In working with a new client, I might encounter a young salesperson who is currently averaging 10 sales per month, and making $50,000 a year. The salesperson wants to join the ranks of the top performers in his field, but doubling his salary overnight would be difficult (if not impossible).

But that doesn't mean the goal is out of reach, just that it needs to be accomplished in steps. Suppose with a bit of coaching and focused effort, the salesperson can start making 12 sales per month, instead of 10, almost immediately. That's a 20% improvement, and one that will make a significant difference in his paycheck. More importantly, though, it sets a new baseline for performance. It establishes a "new normal" that the salesperson can use as an expectation for each month's work. By repeating the process again a few times, he'll be able to get to 15 sales per month, then 18 or 20, and so on…

I gave an example centering on sales because it's a field I know very well and one that lends itself to easy numerical examples that can be imagined in the real world. Really, though, the process of setting and exceeding your own expectations again and again can apply to any profession or situation. All that's required is an idea of what you could accomplish if you tried a little harder and focused yourself a little more, a plan for achieving it, and then the willingness to set new expectations for yourself after you've reached those targets.

This isn't a new or complicated idea — so why don't more people put it to work in their own lives and careers? The sad answer is that they become complacent.

Complacency is the exact opposite of the process of continual improvement that I've been describing here. When you become complacent, you decide that your work – and by extension, the place you've reached in your life – is "good enough." You stop growing and improving.

Why would anyone ever want to do that? In a world of limitless possibilities, why decide to stop moving forward?

I suspect it's because a lot of us mistake happiness with complacency. No matter what your situation, you should do everything you can to feel happy and fulfilled. There's no way to tell what the future will hold, and life is too short to obsess over what you don't have or haven't done. At the same time, though, you should never stop reaching forward. No matter how happy you are now, there's always room for more growth, new frontiers, and bigger achievements. In fact, if you already feel happy, the best way to stay that way isn't to stop, but to keep moving forward.

Who are you right now, and who could you be in the future? The key to bridging those two versions of yourself is to constantly expand and exceed your own expectations.

CHAPTER FIVE

Put in the Time: Work Smarter and Harder

There is a story I hear a lot from other speakers, and have even told myself. It goes something like this: Two lumberjacks are hard at work. The first one chops tirelessly, going from one tree to the next as quickly as he can. The second works hard, too, but takes the occasional break to sit down. At the end of the day, the first lumberjack is astonished to see that the second has cut down more trees than he has.

"How is that possible?" he asks, eyes wide.

"While you were hacking away," the second lumberjack replies, "I was taking breaks to sharpen my axe."

What most people take away from that story can be summed up in a calm expression: Work smarter, not harder. But I think that's only half-right. As important as planning, refinement, and efficiency are, if you want to get ahead in today's world you do need to work smart... but you also need to keep working hard at the same time.

Sharpening up your axe – no matter what that might mean in the context of your day-to-day job – isn't going

"It's not enough

to 'work smart' if you arent
willing to put in the hours. "

to finish the job for you. If there were an app, software automation tool, or simple procedure that could replace your job, you can bet the company you work for would have bought it. Instead, they'll supply you with as many tools as they can to help you get better at what you do, but there's no substitute for a commitment to getting things done if you want to move ahead in your career.

Reaching excellence usually isn't complicated. Modern psychologists say that it takes around 10,000 hours of doing anything to become outstanding at it. But just because something is easy to understand doesn't make it easy to do. You still have to put in the effort, and lots of time, if you want to see the results.

There is a perception, often put forth by advertising that targets young people, that you should be able to have a highly successful career and all the time in the world to hang out in coffee shops, take exotic trips, and pursue multiple hobbies or side projects during all the spare hours you'll find on your calendar. I won't say that's impossible, but it's certainly not an accurate depiction of the way most successful people get their start.

Instead, most of the men and women who make their way to the top begin by learning to work long hours, focus on important goals, *and* improve their efficiency by "working smart." They take classes, learn new software, and add new skills all the time; they just don't do it at the expense of their everyday productivity.

To be clear once again, I'm not saying you should become a workaholic and focus all your energy on your career to the point that you alienate your family and don't enjoy your life. There is a certain balance to achieve, and happiness should be your goal. What I *am* suggesting is that it takes time to become good at anything, and that if you aren't willing to put that time in (particularly early in your career), you aren't going to ever be as happy as you could be because you won't fulfill your potential, won't make it to the top of your organization, and won't ever enjoy the freedom and financial rewards that come with those achievements.

Only you can decide where your priorities lie. I can tell you from experience, though, that your free time feels more free, and can be spent more enjoyably, when you have money, freedom, and a sense of contentment that comes with having achieved something big. Without putting forth a bit of time and effort into your profession, you can't reach the levels of success you aspire to.

It's important to work smart, which is why you need to learn something new every day and always become more efficient in your job or role. But don't be fooled into thinking that there are any shortcuts to the top that don't involve hard work, because it's bound to leave you disappointed and back where you started.

CHAPTER SIX

Know How Your Job Fits into
the Bigger Company Picture

You know what your job title is, but do you know how you fit into your company's bigger plans and/ or profit picture? A surprising number of people don't, and missing that little piece of information can have big implications.

For example, take the cashier working at your favorite fast-food restaurant. In a way, this person's job can be very simple: to greet you, take an order, and then deliver the food. To their employer, however, this person has other tasks that are more important. For instance, if they present themselves professionally and smile, the customer will have a good experience and will be likely to return again. Or if they offer customers a dessert or a larger size soda, they can improve profitability with every sale.

What's important to note here is that, from an employer's perspective, two cashiers who think of themselves as doing a "good job" might be on opposite ends of the spectrum because of the way they fit into the restaurant's overall business plan. And unless they are told or figure out how they

> **Always remember** *that you're part of a team,* *working toward a bigger goal.*

fit into things (which doesn't always happen), their success or failure will seem random.

Let's move to an example that's more common to my work. I'm frequently brought in to present at companies on the subject of customer service. To someone who has been newly hired to handle phone calls, the job of a customer service agent can seem like it consists of fielding angry inquiries and trying to find solutions.

Within most businesses, though, customer service isn't about problems at all... it's about keeping customers (and keeping them happy) at the lowest possible cost. Companies know that it costs a lot of money to find new customers, and so they have to do what they can to keep the ones they've already earned, particularly if they are long-standing accounts. At the same time, spending lots of money on each problem or complaint would quickly destroy the profitability of the business. So they employ customer service agents to find the best balance between those two goals.

For that new hire I mentioned, having that information can be a huge benefit. Instead of guessing at what their priorities should be, and which parts of their performance need to be improved, they can work on finding and nego-tiating low-cost solutions that keep buyers happy. When the focus is shifted from the complaint to the answer, good things happen in that department.

These are just two examples, but the fact of the matter is that I could probably come up with dozens more. That's because millions of people know their job title and basic responsibilities, but have no idea how their work fits into the overall business plan.

No one would pay you to do the things you do if they didn't think it was necessary or beneficial. So your job is to figure out why, even if it seems obvious to you. For instance, an accountant is certainly there to keep the books, but perhaps one of their secondary roles might be to prevent fraud and look for discounts that the business can take advantage of.

Often, you won't be the one to decide what your role is in the business plan. That's actually not necessarily bad news, since it means you can go out and ask someone else. Let them tell you which parts of your job are most important, and which areas of performance affect the business (and the bottom line) most significantly.

As with most of the tips in this book, following this advice can help you in a number of ways. First, it gives you a clear picture of how you'll be evaluated by your supervisors. That can help put you in line for raises, bonuses, and even promotions. It also means you can make yourself more valuable to the business, which is a good way to ensure you'll stick around even if there are cutbacks in the future.

And asking for this kind of information is a good way to keep managers and supervisors happy. After all, the aspects of your job that matter most are the ones that affect them. You can bet they are receiving directives from someone higher up the corporate food chain, so their own bonuses and advancement opportunities are likely dependent on you and your coworkers meeting certain metrics.

If you want to get ahead, it's important to know not just your job, but your role. What is your business trying to do, and how do you fit into the picture?

> *You can get anything you want in life*
> **so long as you are willing**
> *to help other people*
> *get what they want first.*

CHAPTER SEVEN

Remember That People Do Things for Their Reasons, Not Yours

That quote, attributed to the late, great Zig Ziglar, can literally change your life. One of the biggest mistakes you can make in your career is focusing on what you want, and more specifically, assuming that others should know or care about the things you desire.

It doesn't work that way. People don't care about what you want any more than you care about what they want. They will only work with you when your goals intersect – that is, when they can get closer to what they want by helping you to get what you want. In other words, they're going to do things for their reasons, and not yours.

I have spent a great deal of my own career explaining and emphasizing this to others. A new salesperson has to know that the customer won't buy from them just because they want to make a sale; instead, they have to show the customer something they want or need and then let the sale happen as a result. In the same way, no one's going to hand you a bonus, a promotion, or a job offer simply because they think you want or need it... they'll only do it if it helps advance their own interests.

This principle works in small interactions and a bigger overall way. To get colleagues to participate in a presentation, for example, show them how the results are going to save them time, help them earn more money, or otherwise improve things for them. If you want to be promoted, make it clear that you're the right choice for the job because you will create opportunities and remove headaches for the person who will be supervising you.

Or if you are in charge of managing employees and/or vendors, flip things around: Don't ask your team to do things a certain way just because you told them so; give them incentives that coincide with their own plans and hopes instead of asking them to contribute to your success, and give them a path to some reward, or a better future, that also leads to your own goals.

This becomes easier if you understand their goals and personalities in the first place. Some things – like more money, and greater career stability – are nearly universal desires. They are things everyone wants. In other cases, though, it's important to make sure that the reasons or rewards you offer to other people have value to them.

As an example, I often see things like vacations and golf clubs being offered as prizes for performance in sales, customer service, or management. These kinds of gifts can be incentives for some people, but as we'll see in a coming chapter, motivation is a deeply personal thing. If a particular person doesn't really want what you're proposing to give them, then you have a problem because they aren't going to go along with your wishes if they don't see some kind of payoff that matters to them.

You'll notice that I have focused on positive incentives. You can get people to do things for their own reasons while emphasizing the negative (e.g., "Do this or you're fired"), but it only works so often. And when it comes to any period of time lasting for more than a few hours, people tend to be more motivated by what they want than a vague risk of loss. Trying to push too hard can end up being counterproductive.

One of the most fruitless exercises known to man is trying to get another person to do something they just don't want to do, or participate in an activity that they aren't interested in. The harder you try, the more resistant they will become, and the bigger the frustration will be on both sides. No one likes to be ordered or coerced, but everyone likes to be given a chance to move closer to their own goals and dreams.

There are millions of people out there, right now, wondering why others won't just give them what they want out of life, when the reality is they have to earn it by thinking outside themselves and helping others to accomplish their goals, too. Don't make that mistake, because it's a surprisingly easy way to hold yourself back from success.

" **Short-term bursts**
of motivation
can't help you reach
your most important long-term goals "

CHAPTER EIGHT

Motivation is Personal and Ongoing

One of the things I always try to impress upon my students and clients is that people do things for their own reasons, and not yours. Guess what? That applies to you, too.

To put this another way, motivation is incredibly personal. What seems like a big incentive to one person can barely matter to another, and the differences between what will motivate one person versus another can be bigger than you might imagine.

I see this all the time in the companies that I train and consult for. Often, wanting to inspire stronger sales performance, they'll come up with some kind of contest where the prize might be an exotic vacation. That's a good idea, in theory, but the fact of the matter is that some people don't really want to spend a week in a tropical destination. And even giving them the cash equivalent might not work.

For instance, it's widely assumed that money is a universal motivator, but that's simply not true… especially after a certain point. Some individuals aren't nearly as motivated by money as they are the desire to have friends, knowledge, and prestige. Others want money, but only because it "buys" them more personal power. And there are even people who will stop being motivated by money after they reach a certain level of comfort or income.

This isn't just a problem for managers and human resources directors looking for new ways to get employees to do more – the minute you stop feeling motivated, you greatly decrease the odds that you'll be able to fulfill your career potential.

In order to be motivated, you have to know what motivates you. In other words, you have to examine your own feelings and desires to find a goal that *really* drives you forward. No one else can give you this inspiration — it's much more powerful if it comes from within. Without a strong emotional element, motivation will always feel fleeting.

Another thing you have to remember about motivation is that your drive and ambition need to be reinforced over time. Attending a seminar, or listening to an audio clip, might make you motivated for a little while. After some period of time, though, that message is going to seem less fresh and relevant, especially when you're confronted with day-to-day habits and struggles. Therefore, you need a way to continue pushing yourself forward when things get tough.

Luckily, there is one answer to both of these problems. To make your success seem personal and exciting, and to motivate yourself over time, you just need to follow a two-step plan. The first is to think about what your dreams are, both for the short term and the long term. Don't just think about what you want to have, buy, or do, but also what you want to be over the coming weeks, months, and years. Give this some serious thought and write your answers down.

Next, find a way to reinforce those desires again and again. For example, one very popular technique is to create a "goal board" or scrapbook with pictures of the things you would love to have or achieve inside. By looking at it each morning, you remind yourself of what you're working toward and keep your goals fresh and firmly planted in your mind.

A similar way to keep yourself motivated is to develop a series of affirmations that you read to yourself a few times each day. It might seem silly, but saying something like "I'll soon be making $100,000 a year" aloud, again and again, has a powerful subconscious effect. It builds a sense of belief in yourself, and sets your mind toward working out details instead of obsessing over obstacles.

There are other things you can do to stay motivated, of course, like spending time with successful people. We will cover several of them in the remaining chapters of this book. For the moment, I just want you to remember that you might not be motivated by the same kinds of goals as other people, and that's perfectly fine. Or you might want the proverbial tropical vacation, but there could be other goals that inspire you even more.

Take the time to figure out what really moves you to action, and then develop a method for reminding yourself about your goals every day. Success involves a lot of hard work, and it's much, much easier to persevere when you remember that motivation has to be personal and ongoing.

CHAPTER NINE

To Be the Best, Spend Time with the Best

In many ways, you are the company you keep. That's not just an old axiom; it's a verifiable truth, reinforced by one study after another over the course of decades. If you hang out with ambitious, educated, wealthy people, you are dramatically more likely to join their ranks than you would be if you spend time with people who aren't going anywhere in life.

For someone who wants to make their way to the top, this should lead to an obvious conclusion: *If you want to be the best, spend your time with the best.*

This principle works for a few different reasons. On the most basic level, spending time with others who are excellent in their work gives you the chance to observe them, learn how they do it, and even pick up their habits. It's amazing how much you can take in, both consciously and unconsciously, just by being around someone who seems to know exactly what they are doing in their work and career.

"*Excellence is contagious.*

Are you hanging out with people who are motivated and positive? "

The second reason to spend time with successful people is that ambition and enthusiasm are contagious. When you're around others who are excited about life, and their careers, you start to be excited, too. The world seems full of new possibilities, and you start to witness the different ways that positive, creative thinking can turn into action and then results.

As I've written so many times before, success is largely about attitude, and there's no better way to cultivate a great attitude than by spending time with lots of people who are in a positive frame of mind. It just rubs off on you in a good way.

Also, when you spend time with a lot of successful people, something magical starts to happen: You stop seeing them as being impossibly talented and start to recognize them for being the hard workers that they are. In other words, you no longer feel the need to delude yourself with the myth that you can't make it because you don't have the right look, education, or last name.

I've been around long enough to know that, while some of us undoubtedly *do* get a head start in life, those who are working the hardest and committing the most just about always make it to the top. That's a big realization, especially if you feel stuck on the idea that you might not have what it takes to succeed. Find top performers in virtually any business or industry and you'll discover that many of them are just people, like you and me, who have kept at it for a long time.

Millions of people fail to reach their potential because they think they don't have what it takes, or that they can never fulfill their dreams because they don't have the right connections. There is a small grain of truth in this – you often *do* need good connections if you want to accomplish something extraordinary. Those connections aren't made at country clubs and alumni meetings, though; they are forged through common ambition.

In other words, by making a point to be around successful people, you are *already* making the connections that will make you more successful in the future. By associating with others who have drive and ambition, you are stacking the deck in your favor.

There are a lot of ways to surround yourself with positive, successful individuals. In some ways, it might happen naturally just from following other pieces of good advice, like pursuing additional skills and education. When you attend night classes related to your career, for example, you're bound to run into others who also see possibilities and are on the way up.

Finding a mentor is another good way to get some of that influence. Often, accomplished individuals like to further their legacy by helping others to succeed or continue their work. This is something we'll explore in a coming chapter.

If all else fails, you can also do something so traditional that it seems unconventional these days: Find someone who has the kind of success you'd like to have, introduce yourself, and spend some time with them. Most people will be flattered, and will be happy to work with you if you show a little ambition (remember, they want to spend time with positive, successful people, too).

To be the best in your field, and realize your true potential, spend time with other people who are either at the top of their game or working their way up. It's one of the best success habits you can ever cultivate.

"Never forget that someone else would love **to have the chances** *you've already gotten.*"

CHAPTER TEN

Someone Else Wants Your Job

There are a lot of things that hold people back from success, but the worst might also be one of the easiest to fall for: *complacency.*

It's human nature to become comfortable, and to stop seeing threats and harmful surroundings when we become accustomed to a certain routine. This can be harmful in any part of your life, with the tendency to take a spouse or loved one for granted being an obvious and common example. At work, though, it can be a career-killer.

In a broad sense, getting complacent means you stop growing, stop pushing yourself forward, and stop maximizing your opportunities. That's enough to ensure that you'll never reach your dreams. But it could also mean that you'll eventually find yourself unemployed with few good prospects.

Make no mistake: *Someone else wants your job.* In fact, the better your job is, the more people there are – in your city, within your industry, and around the world – who would like to take it from you.

That should be reason enough to always be improving and making yourself more useful. Just because you have your position today doesn't mean you'll always have it. Remember, even if you don't think much of your job now, you probably saw it as a big opportunity once. That means it's probably still a good opportunity for lots of people.

If it seems like I'm trying to scare you a little bit, you can thank me later. A small amount of fear and paranoia can be very valuable to your career. You don't want to spend every minute looking over your shoulder, of course, but you shouldn't forget there are others behind you who want what you have, either.

This applies just as strongly to any job you want in the future, by the way. Not only do you have competitors who would gladly step into your chair and show what they can do, but there even *more* people who want to be your boss, earn big money, and make it to the corner office. A lot of them won't have the drive needed to get there, but the ones who do deserve a little bit of your consideration.

They have the same dreams and goals you do, the same work ethic, and the same number of hours in a day. It's up to you to figure out what you can do to separate yourself and stay ahead of them. Is it going to be your education, the unique skill set, your talents as a leader, or something else?

Give it some thought, because they'll be trying to maximize their strengths, too.

I always like to remind ambitious people that there isn't as much competition at the top of any field, but anyone who is willing to work relentlessly for their own success has to be taken seriously. You can never assume that you're the natural choice for promotion, or that your career is going to work out just because you've taken all the "standard" steps to reach the level you aspire to.

In today's unpredictable world, businesses are looking for creative, focused people who can get results. If you're one of them, there's no limit to how far you can go and what you'll be able to accomplish. On the other hand, if you're just treading water, in your job and your career, you'd better keep a close eye on your rearview mirror.

Somebody out there wants your job, and if you aren't willing to keep improving yourself and growing your skill set, it's only a matter of time before they come and take it from you.

*" The interview doesn't end when you're hired... at least not if you **want to keep moving up.** "*

CHAPTER ELEVEN

Always Be Interviewing for Your Next Job

I'm going to assume, if you're reading this, that you haven't already reached your dream job. You might be successful already, but you are hoping to find even more success in the future. Or maybe you are starting at the bottom and working your way up. You could even be "stuck" in a position and don't know how to move forward.

Regardless of the specific circumstances, I have a good piece of advice I hope you'll consider: *Always be interviewing for your next job.*

I don't mean this literally. Although you should keep an eye out for new opportunities, whether they're in your organization or another one, going on an endless cycle of interviews isn't going to do much for you. It takes valuable time away from your current position and career, and it won't take long for word to get around if you seem like you're job-hopping from one organization to the next.

What I'm advising instead is that you always be actively campaigning for advancement in your company or industry.

I'm suggesting you treat your work as an ongoing interview that's going to lead to something bigger.

How do you do that? The first step is to present yourself as a professional. Dress, as the old adage goes, for the job you want instead of the job you have. Cultivate good manners, if you don't have them already, and be pleasant and professional when you deal with managers, coworkers, and colleagues.

Naturally, putting in a strong performance in your current job is always a good idea. It causes supervisors to think of you favorably, and helps you establish a good track record with your company, customers, coworkers, and even other contacts in and around your business. Nothing builds a reputation like good work.

Another way to "interview" for your next job is to make sure that the right people know you'd like to move up. You need to be a little strategic about this, of course, so you don't give off the impression of wanting to replace your boss a few weeks after being hired to your current position. But without going into specifics, you can present yourself as being vaguely ambitious, and let others around you know that you would like to do bigger things for yourself in the future, even if that future isn't right away.

By reinforcing that message from time to time, you'll accomplish two important things. First, you'll build a circle of people who know that you're looking to grow in your career and make it more likely that you'll hear about new opportunities as they come up. And second, you'll signal to them that you are available for new projects and responsibilities, which could entail more work in the short term but bigger chances in the future. That way, when it's time to hire or promote, your name will be one of the first to come up.

Of course, you can't actually interview for your next job until you have the right qualifications. So it's important to cultivate the right skills, experience, and certifications so you'll be ready to move up when the time is right.

A surprising number of people don't even know where their next opportunity for advancement would lead. You can't get the job you want if you don't know what it is, so take the time to study a few realistic options. Find out where you could go from where you're at right now, and what education, qualities, or specific skills you would have to have to make that leap. Then, get to work on adding them to your résumé.

The great thing about each of these tactics is that they don't require anything special, except an awareness of where you're at in your career and where you'd like to go. From there, you just start putting different pieces into place and making yourself a stronger candidate. Eventually, when the right opening comes along, you'll already have everything you need, including contacts who can recommend you for the job. At that point, your actual interview should be easy.

Treat your work as if you're always being evaluated for a new opportunity. That's closer to the reality of your career than you might realize, and it's a perfect way to position yourself for success.

" *We all have the same*
number of hours each day.
It's how you use them
that counts.
"

CHAPTER TWELVE

To Master Success, Master Time Management

You have something in common with the CEO of your company, the billionaires you read about in the business press, and even the president of the United States of America... and, for that matter, every person who is more successful or less successful than you are. Each of you gets the same 24 hours in a day.

This isn't a new realization, but it's an important one. Because how you spend those 24 hours is the one thing that will determine whether you ever reach your goals or not.

Far too often, time management is thought of as something that you learn about in a seminar and then forget, or a soft skill that's all about learning how to conduct high-impact meetings while you're sitting on the freeway. I don't think either of those notions is correct, or particularly helpful.

My definition of time management would be "being intentional about how you spend your day." With that frame of mind, you can finish a 12-hour work day and only cross one item off your to-do list, spend a few hours reading a book about your business, or even take the day off to spend time with a loved one and be "productive" because it's moving you toward your goals and the life you want to live. I know, because I've done all three on several different occasions.

Good time management is about *effectiveness*, not just *efficiency*. In other words, it involves thinking about what you want to get done, and not just the rate at which you are doing it. You can be plenty busy, day after day, getting lots of things finished and going nowhere in your career. And you can concentrate on a few key tasks, finishing them one at a time, and find tremendous success.

Time management is such a huge topic that I couldn't even begin to fully address it in a short chapter. For that reason, I recommend that you check out a few good books and seminars on the subject, including my own. In the meantime, I'm going to leave you with a few simple ideas that also happen to be life- and career-changing.

The first is that you *have* to know how you're spending your time. Try keeping a time log and record how you spend your day in half-hour increments. No one will see the finished log except you, so don't feel the need to cheat or exaggerate. If you worked for three hours and then spent two hours on lunch and coffee, write it down.

What you'll probably find, if you're like most people, is that you're spending a lot of time on things that don't truly matter. They might seem urgent, but they aren't moving you toward your long-term goals. That's a problem.

Armed with that insight, you should find a way to make time for the activities that are going to bring you closer to your dreams. Whether you need to take a class, spearhead a new project, or write a report, figure out what the next step is and set aside the minutes or hours you need to get started. Come in to work early, take a few files home with you, or do whatever else is needed to set aside a little bit of uninterrupted quiet time every day to make progress. Those chunks of time will add up, and you'll suddenly find yourself moving closer to your dreams than ever before.

Next, figure out when you do your best work. Ask yourself: When do you feel energized and creative, and which parts of the day make you feel like you're struggling the most? Try to line up those important tasks you've identified with the parts of your schedule that are most conducive to concentration.

And finally, learn to concentrate on important core tasks by taking on less. That doesn't mean neglecting the parts of your job that are mandatory, just that you should get good at delegating (that is, simply saying "no") so you can concentrate your energy on things that matter a great deal. Most of your day should be taken up by activities that either determine how effectively you perform your job or position you to take advantage of other opportunities in the future.

It is incredibly easy to let time slip away, especially if you aren't paying attention. I encourage you to learn more about time management on your own. Keep learning, in fact, until you feel like you've developed a system that works for you and you're more productive than ever.

Until that happens, work on using these habits I've given you and see the profound difference they can make in your career.

CHAPTER THIRTEEN

Practice Getting Comfortable in Front of a Group

Success comes in a lot of different shapes and sizes, as does talent. But there are a few traits that top-performing men and women almost always share. One of them is an ability to comfortably speak and present to groups.

Being a strong public speaker is one of those skills that's massively important, even though the reasons why aren't always obvious. Believe me when I tell you that few things can open up your potential as much as being able to stand in front of a room full of strangers and have your ideas be heard.

One reason that being able to present is so important to your career advancement has to do with simple math. No matter how likable and competent you seem in a person-to-person interaction, the limits of time mean that you can only interact directly with so many individuals on a daily and weekly basis. The more in-depth your ideas are, the longer

"When you can speak to groups,
your power as a leader
and influencer multiples."

they take to explain, and the less time you have left to work with other people.

When you have confidence as a public speaker, on the other hand, you can transmit that same knowledge, belief, and enthusiasm to dozens, hundreds, or even thousands of other people at once... and all without taking more of your time. Instead of building support for your project or career on an individual basis, you can do it in a group.

A more subtle reason to work on your public speaking skills has to do with credibility. Human beings are inherently wired to follow leaders. And we associate leadership (at least to some small degree) with the confidence in guiding groups. So when you come off impressively in front of a lot of people, the effect is that much stronger. Your credibility as a leader in your company or field is enhanced simply because you have presented to lots of people at the same time.

It should also be noted that, as I always like to remind students and readers, enthusiasm is contagious. If you can get a few people excited about what you have to say in a group, you'll have an easier time getting others to be excited about it too. Group dynamics make that possible, and can be important for swaying certain high-level individuals.

For example, suppose you want to launch a new project that greatly increases your visibility within your business and represents a major career milestone. It's going to cost a lot of money, though, and your budget-conscious CFO is unlikely to support the plan. By presenting it in a group, and getting *lots* of people excited about it at once, you can influence this person's thinking (and bring them around to your point of view) in a way that might be difficult or even impossible in a one-on-one meeting.

With all these benefits, it's a wonder that *everyone* isn't a master public speaker. As we all know, however, lots of individuals have a natural fear of talking in front of groups.

If you're one of them, or just don't feel like a very polished speaker, then I've got some good news for you: Becoming a strong presenter is all about practice, and overcoming a few bad habits. I've written a short book on the topic – my 5 POWER Presentation Steps – so I won't go into endless detail here. What I will tell you, though, is that most people find that their nervousness about public speaking melts away once they've had the right preparation. When you know what you want to say, and why, and have practiced speaking in front of groups, your confidence rises pretty quickly.

Even if you don't foresee a need to do any public speaking in the near future, I encourage you to join a group, take a class, or otherwise find a way to give it a try. For one thing, you might find that you like presenting to groups and are naturally good at it. And for another, I can guarantee that you'll eventually come to some point in your career where it will be a necessary skill if you want to advance. Why not master it now and be well on your way?

CHAPTER FOURTEEN

Pay Attention to Your Personal Brand and Reputation

What do the people you work with say about you when you're not around? What kinds of impressions do supervisors, coworkers, and customers have about you and your professionalism?

Even if you don't know, you can probably guess. That's because you know what kind of employee and colleague you are, whether you can be considered dependable, hard-working, and someone who follows through on their word.

Those impressions essentially amount to your reputation, which could also be thought of as your "personal brand." And it plays a large part in determining what kinds of opportunities come (or don't come) your way.

Large corporations spend billions on branding because they know it can have a huge effect on things like sales and recruiting. Even when we aren't doing it consciously, humans make snap, split-second decisions about what we'll

> *The impressions other people*
> *have about you*
> **can make or break**
> *your career.*

pay attention to, which products we'll buy, and whom we will or won't trust. "Branding" is just a term we've invented to think more carefully about those impressions, and it can apply to an individual person in the same way it can an organization or logo.

Stop and think about the three people who work the closest to you in your office or department. How do they dress and speak? Do they tend to be on time, or habitually late? Would you think of them as sharp and ambitious, or slow and complacent?

These are all examples of personal branding and reputation. Knowing that, flip things around and ask yourself: *How would those three people answer the same questions about you?*

The best way to enjoy a strong personal brand is to cultivate it. That is, don't leave things to chance. There are always going to be some individuals who will like you, and some who won't, but there should never be any question of whether they respect you or consider you to be competent in the things you do.

And so, as with so many things, growing a good reputation starts with the basics like showing up to work on time, presenting yourself professionally, and learning to be one of the best at your job.

Beyond that, cultivating a strong personal brand is like mounting a successful public relations campaign. You have to make sure that people are aware of you, and talking about you, but also that they are saying the right things.

A good starting point is to simply make sure you know influential people, both within your company's walls and without. Nobody likes a person who brags endlessly, but we all notice the compliments and kind words given by others. If you want to build the right kind of reputation, form good relationships, be nice to others you work with, and present yourself as a generally cheerful and competent person, learn to follow up on your promises and avoid making excuses. The people around you will notice and spread your reputation for you.

Also remember that many people will hear of you or about you before they ever meet you. Anything you can do to increase your visibility within your field – like writing reports that are posted online, for example, or keeping an active profile on business-related websites – helps to establish your reputation.

It's easy to derail that kind of effort, in the digital age, by sending the wrong things through email or posting them online to your social media accounts. You might not like it that your coworkers (not to mention future employers) can learn about your life from the things you put on the Internet, but that's a fact of modern life. That doesn't mean you have to be a robot who never shares a joke or has a political point of view, just that you should be aware that anything you add to the Internet can potentially be seen by everyone you know and can help or hurt your personal brand.

That brings us to another important point: Don't forget to check up on your own reputation from time to time. Google your own name, visit your personal website, and take care to notice what others might be saying or sharing online that might add to or take away from your reputation.

At some point, a client, recruiter, or executive is going to have to make a decision about whether they should take a chance on working with you or not. One of the first things they'll do is reach out to their own contacts and try to get a little more information about you and your work. When that happens, your personal brand and reputation are going to either open or close the door to that opportunity. Will you be ready?

Texting is quick and convenient, but it's not always **personal or effective.**

CHAPTER FIFTEEN

Add a Personal Touch to Your Texting

To say that technology has changed the way we communicate over the years that I've been training and presenting would be the understatement of the century. When I was fresh out of school, we got by with mailed letters, phone calls, and face-to-face meetings. Now, many of the same conversations are conducted by text, email, and video chat.

Don't worry: I'm not going to be one of those people who thinks Western civilization is going to fall because we're always on our phones. I think texting and other forms of digital messaging are incredibly convenient; I couldn't get through my day without them.

What I *will* tell you, though, is that relationships make and break careers, and that you need to be sure you add a personal touch to your communications. In other words, don't try to get by on texts and emoticons alone.

Texting and email are, in many ways, the communications equivalent of fast food. They get the job done, but they aren't necessarily fulfilling or rewarding. To be clear once again, that doesn't make them bad... it just means they aren't necessarily enough, either.

Experts estimate that more than 80% of human communication is expressed non-verbally. In other words, what we say (or in many cases, type) is actually the *subtext* of what we mean. Take that subtext away, and you still have information, but not any emotion.

This leaves the door open to misunderstandings, of course – everyone has had the experience of being misinterpreted through email, or having an autocorrected text change the tone of what they were trying to convey – but also to interactions that feel empty. In case you're wondering, this isn't just for older people, but also younger ones, too. We all want to feel like we are getting to know others, and being understood in the process.

Knowing this, you can help your career in a few critical ways. The first is to become a better electronic communicator. If you can learn to text in more complete sentences, and without all but the most common abbreviations, it can decrease the odds that you'll be misunderstood and make you seem like more of a polished professional. The same goes for email, where rambling messages and misspellings can undermine your credibility.

Whenever you are communicating online, remember that you're trying to establish yourself as a professional with a solid reputation. Take the few extra seconds to type something coherent and don't leave room for someone to take an idea or suggestion the wrong way.

At the same time, you should realize that the increase in digital communication has made real, genuine, face-to-face contact more valuable. In the same way that email has made handwritten personal letters feel more "genuine" than a quick note dashed off from a PC, the rise of texting and video chats has made an actual in-person get-together seem more important.

There is also a different energy level when you see someone face-to-face than there would be at a great distance. Everything feels more personal, and it's easier to pick up on small verbal and physical cues.

With that knowledge, you should look to make the most of every communication. For simple, everyday interactions, decrease your time commitment by emailing or texting. Better yet, create pre-written templates so you can dash a note off in seconds and keep up your professional image.

On the other hand, when the stakes are high or a relationship is being built and nurtured, emphasize personal contact. Make the time and effort to simply "be there," because it shows colleagues and customers that you care, and they have your full attention.

It's ironic that the convenience of the digital age has made authentic communication more difficult than it was in the past, but that's the world we live in. Texts, emails, and other forms of instant messaging aren't going away, and we shouldn't want them to. At the same time, however, never forget that it takes a personal touch to build a real relationship, and the strongest relationships are the ones that are going to help you grow and sustain your career.

CHAPTER SIXTEEN

Make the Right Investments (in Yourself)

I t would be impossible to estimate how many millions or billions of pages are generated each and every year on the subject of good investing. And yet, a lot of professionals miss out on genuine opportunities to grow, make more money, and generate solid business connections because they never make the one investment that always pays off: the one they make in themselves.

If you want a top-shelf career, you're going to have to invest some of what you make back into your own potential. Those investments can take a lot of different forms, but many fall into the category of education and efficiency.

The value of education is probably something you've heard all your life, and in many ways it's self-explanatory. If you wake up smarter tomorrow than you were today, you can probably find a way to make more money or improve your career because of it. Likewise, as you take on new skills, you

> *The investments you make in yourself are the ones that* **pay back the most.**

also expand your value and generate new opportunities out of thin air.

Efficiency isn't thought of as often, but it's just as straightforward. If you purchase a piece of software, for example, that allows you to do some important aspect of your job 20% faster, then you can either increase your productivity or find more time for other tasks and projects. The same could be said for apps, books, training courses, and other career-oriented purchases.

In some cases, simply spending money on what you want can be good for your on-the-job performance. An easy way to understand this is by thinking about something like an expensive office chair that reduces back pain and fatigue. Such a purchase might seem extravagant until you consider that it's going to allow you to get more work done, or show up at the office feeling happy and refreshed.

Other examples of investing in yourself could include buying a ticket to a motivational seminar, having a suit professionally tailored, or working with a career coach who can help you overcome fears and identify your longer-term goals. It could be lunch with a mentor, or a few dollars spent on an alarm clock that forces you to get out of bed and come to the office early so you can work on an important project without being interrupted.

As you might have guessed from the examples I've given so far, there really aren't any perfect guidelines when it comes to investing in yourself. In fact, even time off – in the form of a vacation or retreat – can represent a "good investment" if it refreshes your mind, even though it won't lead to future earnings directly.

Knowing that the concept of investing in yourself and your own career is something that's hard to pin down, I recommend you simply take a certain percentage of your income, set it aside, and then ask yourself: "How could I be getting better at my job, or closer to my career goals?" In some cases, the answers won't cost you anything. But if they do, you'll already have a little bit of money set aside.

Don't be afraid to spend a little bit of money on yourself, especially if it's going to lead to more opportunities in the long run. The most successful people always bet on themselves, and make smart investments that increase their knowledge and efficiency.

In a certain sense, each and every one of us is a "one-person business," relying on our own skills, talents, and productivity to generate income year after year. Why not make sure that some of your money is going toward that goal so your personal company can always be getting stronger and more profitable?

CHAPTER SEVENTEEN

Nurture Your Comic Side

Despite the fact that a few people would refer to their workplaces as being "comical," I have found again and again that a healthy sense of humor can be a real asset to your career. This probably shouldn't be a big surprise, as humor is an excellent icebreaker, and knowing a few jokes is one of the easiest ways to make an impression on others in social settings.

This is true even if you aren't a professional speaker and trainer, like I am. I've seen salespeople, customer service agents, and managers all diffuse tension, and get others to listen to what they have to say, by opening with something funny. And of course, if you want to learn to speak to groups, having a funny bone doesn't hurt.

For a lot of people, humor comes naturally. If that's the case for you, then nurture your comic side a bit by memorizing a few (clean) jokes and learning to spot the humor in everyday situations. On the other hand, if you

" *Business is a serious business...*
or is it? "

aren't naturally that funny, try to grow that side of your personality a bit. It's probably easier than you think – a joke can sometimes be even *funnier* if it comes from a person you wouldn't expect to tell one.

If you want to go a bit farther, there are lots of ways to nurture your inner comedian. You could always sign up for improv classes, or an open mic night, to earn some experience getting laughs. Or for a lower-key approach, you could make a habit of renting comedic movies once a week or two to get a sense of pace and timing.

The risk in using humor to grow your career is that you'll either go too far or make the wrong remark at the wrong time. Even though a bit of humor is almost always welcome, there are some things you just can't joke about in today's workplace. I'm not going to bother listing them here; instead, use common sense. If you think there's a chance someone will be offended by what you're about to laugh about, then skip making the joke.

Also, remember that there's a time and place for everything. No one wants to hear your latest wisecrack when a manager is talking about layoffs, or your coworker is going through a serious illness. Context is everything.

You shouldn't let those warnings deter you, though. Once you get a sense of what kinds of jokes you can safely make at work, and how to deliver them, it can be a big boost for your interpersonal skills. I know of at least a few people who are often invited to closed meetings and executive retreats just because they know how, and when, to lighten the mood a little bit. When you have a good sense of humor, you are easier to be around and you come off as a more confident person.

Comedy opens doors and paves the way for new interactions and relationships to form. It grabs people's attention, gives them a better opinion of you, and makes them more likely to listen to what you have to offer... even if that's bad news or a promotional pitch. Everyone likes to be entertained, and humor is one of the most universal forms of entertainment you'll ever find.

That being said, comedy isn't easy. I can tell you from experience that learning a joke and delivering it successfully are two different things, and that it's very easy to overstep the mark and say something you shouldn't. Remember that, and don't try to turn yourself into a barrel of laughs overnight. Just remember that having a good sense of humor and getting others to laugh can be a great asset to your career. Then, use your spare moments to hone that skill so you can pull it out when it's appropriate.

CHAPTER EIGHTEEN

Take Advantage of Mentorship

Wouldn't it be nice if you knew someone who had been in your shoes, faced the same problems you're dealing with, and knew the answers from personal experience?

Chances are, you already do... or could, if you're willing to look for them. And they would be happy to share their wisdom with you, if only you would take the time to find them and ask.

Of all the things you can do to help build a successful career, finding a mentor is one of the easiest *and* one of the most overlooked. There are literally thousands, and maybe tens of thousands, of men and women who could help you to chart a strategy for the future and overcome difficulties because they have more experience in your industry (and in life) than you do. But most of us never take the time to seek them out and learn what they have to offer.

"Mentors have experience
you don't, and
perspective you need."

I've been fortunate to have several mentors in my own life. Almost all of the very successful people I work with have had at least a few good mentors, too. If you're not getting any guidance and advice from somebody else, now is the perfect time to ask why.

Finding a mentor isn't usually difficult. All it takes is a willingness to go to industry events, or seek out someone in your company who is farther along than you are, and see if they'd be willing to share some of what they've learned. You don't have to ask them to be a formal mentor, and most people will be so flattered by the request that they'll be glad to help. At a minimum, they'll probably be open to meeting with you once or twice a year to talk about specific situations, or your career in general.

The one thing you have to be sure of is that you choose your mentor wisely. Ideally, you want someone who has had a great deal of success, is a good listener, and would like to see you succeed. The last thing you want is a mentor who doesn't want to see you do well or has bad habits they could pass on.

It's not a terrible idea to have several mentors, especially if you aren't meeting with them on a very regular basis. The more perspectives you have, the more you can learn. And it's less of a time commitment for each of your mentors if you're meeting with a handful of them at regular intervals.

Once you have a mentor, or several, just take the time to meet with them and ask questions. You can always steer the conversation toward a problem or issue that you're facing, but your main goal should be to let them speak. In time, they'll give you valuable insights – many of which you can use to become happier and more productive.

Don't forget that this is a door that swings both ways. In the same way that you want to find others who can serve as mentors to you, you should be open to helping out those who are trying to achieve what you already have. Even an entry-level employee can serve as a mentor to students and interns, and you'd be surprised at what you know that you could share with others.

The key word in that idea is "surprise." While most people think of knowledge as flowing from the mentor to the protégé, the reality is that both parties benefit. I know, from having been in each role, that you can learn and grow just as much through the process of giving advice as you can from taking it. Sometimes, others will ask questions that cause you to change your thinking or stumble onto a new idea. At the very least, serving as a mentor to someone else exposes you to fresh ideas and makes you appreciate how far you've come in your career.

Both having a mentor and serving as one are great ways to add to your knowledge and perspective. So make a point to get out there and meet others who have the kind of success you want. And then, share what you've learned with someone else.

CHAPTER NINETEEN

Get Away for a Fresh Perspective

Sometimes, the very best thing you can do for your job performance, and your career in general, is to just ignore it for a little while. That's because getting away – for a few days, a week, or even longer – can be just what's needed to relax, refresh your mind, and see pressing problems with a new perspective.

Note that what I'm recommending here isn't a simple afternoon away from the office, or the kind of evening and weekend activities that most of us would consider essential to "work/life balance." Those leisurely and social outings are important, but I'm talking about something that takes you away from your normal surroundings, out of your everyday comfort zone, and into an environment where you are forced to get away from your normal habits and thought patterns.

The easiest way to accomplish that is by traveling. In fact, the farther you can go, and the longer you can stay away (within reasonable limits), the better it will probably be

"*Want to help your career?*
Ignore it for a week or two.

for your perspective and mental health. A weekend spent in a new city can stop you from going over the same ideas and roadblocks in your mind; two or three weeks spent in another country can alter the way you view your entire life or business.

Best of all, you probably won't have to do anything to "force" a mental breakthrough. You just need to get away long enough to stop thinking about the things that are typically on your mind. From there, your brain will take over and start filling in gaps, and making new connections, while you are actively pursuing other thoughts or activities. It works almost like magic – one minute you're taking photos or collecting seashells, and the next minute you realize you have a new customer retention strategy.

The idea of renewing yourself by changing your surroundings isn't a new one. Writers, philosophers, and artists have known for centuries that a change of scenery can be the cure for any type of creative block. And as you've probably figured out by now, I consider most parts of business to be creative endeavors, as well, even if a lot of business people don't think about their jobs that way.

Even though taking a vacation is the easiest (and most fun) way to give yourself a mental refresher, there are other options. For instance, you might be able to get a break from your everyday routine by attending a conference, going on a retreat, or even signing up for some kind of specialized training that takes place away from your home and office.

That kind of travel offers a different challenge for your mind, but can be just as beneficial (especially when you consider that you'll be learning new skills, and probably surrounded by others who can motivate you, serve as mentors, etc.). Identifying these opportunities can be as simple as checking a few websites to see what's going on in your business or industry.

Ironically enough, the biggest obstacle to getting away probably isn't your employer or your schedule. While it's true that Americans get fewer vacation days than workers in most other places around the world, it's also true that we tend to not even use the majority of what we are given. That's particularly true at the top, where driven people tend to worry that taking long vacations will "set them back" in their careers.

In reality, traveling often has the opposite effect. Vacations, as well as the conferences and retreats we attend, inspire creativity, let us reflect on the progress we've made, and even form the basis for new projects and partnerships with the people we meet.

It has never been easier or more affordable to get out there and see the world. Taking time off might seem like a terrible way to get ahead in your job, but it could give you incredible benefits – and satisfaction – over the course of your career.

CHAPTER TWENTY

Become the Expert in Your Field

How would you like to enjoy rock-solid job security, a salary that's more than any of your peers earn, and worldwide respect within your industry? You can have all of that, and more, simply by becoming *the* expert in your field or community.

Those who make it to the top are always experts. They might not have extensive degrees, or think of themselves as having extensive technical knowledge, but they are experts nonetheless. Some are experts at finding and keeping new customers. Others are experts in cutting costs and building relationships. Still more are experts in technology, logistics, or manufacturing processes. There are even others like me who are experts in training and motivation.

It doesn't matter what your particular specialty is. Experts who can help a business expand its reach, make more money, or enjoy a healthier bottom line are always going to be in demand. That's because companies have

> *Employees are replaceable, but* **experts are always in demand.**

problems and challenges they need to solve, and when they do, they want a person with knowledge and experience who can show them the way forward.

Becoming the expert in your field is easier than you probably think. The first step is to think about what your field actually is, in the most specific way possible. For example, lots of people are "experts" in restaurant management, but I'd be willing to bet there are two or three people who know more than anyone else about franchising fast food restaurants in the South. You could turn up dozens of experts on web design just by looking online, but a search for the ultimate authority on e-commerce security would probably yield very few names.

These are just examples, but I could go on and on for different industries and niches. The fact is that there are always a few people at the top who have the *knowledge* and *recognition* needed to be considered the preeminent experts in their fields.

Because I want you to be the expert in your field, it's important that we take a slightly closer look at those two key terms. You can't be considered the authority on what you do – and get the recognition and pay that come with it – without those two key ingredients.

Acquiring knowledge is relatively straightforward, but it takes time. In some cases, more traditional education might be required, but more often than not, gaining mastery of a subject is more dependent on focus than it is credentials.

You can be the expert in reducing customer service costs for your industry, for example, without having an MBA. People value experience and specialized knowledge over degrees when dollars and cents are on the line.

That brings us to the second quality of an expert, which is recognition. It doesn't matter if you know more about your field than anyone else on earth – if others don't know that fact, they aren't going to turn to you for help.

Therefore, it's up to you to share your knowledge and (tastefully) promote yourself regularly. This could involve writing papers and reports, holding seminars within your company, or even submitting articles to industry journals and composing entire books. Each of these projects takes time, focus, and continual learning, but they all pay off significantly. Once you've led a few discussions on the subject, or published a few works that others can find and download, you'll be amazed at how quickly you become recognized as someone who knows your topic inside and out.

Once you achieve that kind of status and recognition as a leading authority, your career starts to take on an entirely new dimension. Instead of having to look for promotions and new opportunities, you'll find that others start seeking you out because of what you know and how it can help them. You become a known quantity and a proven problem-solver; that's a valuable commodity in today's world, no matter what field you're in.

Most business people would like to be experts, but aren't willing to take the time needed to learn and master a field or discipline. That's too bad, because experts are the ones who have the most to offer and the least to worry about. And it doesn't take much effort to *stay* an expert after you already become one, because you've already mastered the basic ideas and fundamentals.

Will you be the next authority in your field?

" **To create the success**
you want, <u>you</u> have to
build it <u>your</u> way. "

CHAPTER TWENTY ONE

Find Your Own Blueprint for Success

Contrary to what you might believe, there are a lot of different kinds of people who create success for themselves. Not everyone who achieves their dreams is a hard-driven, type-A personality who works tirelessly from the crack of dawn until the late hours of the evening. In fact, the whole idea of "success" is deeply personal, and the prestige or financial rewards that matter to one person aren't necessarily the goal for another.

That's something I stress several times through this book, but it's worth repeating here because you should now have the advice you need to take the next step and start getting more from your life. But you still have to take those steps yourself, and decide on your own what you actually want to be getting out of that life.

One of the easiest ways to find yourself tired and un-fulfilled is to attempt to duplicate someone else's success. Studying the path that another person has taken, and duplicating it, can be helpful if you're feeling stuck, or like you don't have any direction. Before long, though, you'll have to branch out onto your own path and find what works for you.

As part of my work in coaching and consulting for my business clients, I'm often called upon to perform personality assessments that reveal tendencies, habits, and motivations in individuals. Sometimes, these qualities are so hidden that the interviewees themselves don't even know they exist. And yet, once they are shown the results, they often become thoughtful and acknowledge that, *yes*, the report really *does* show how they tend to think, act, and feel.

Do yourself a favor and don't try to live another person's life. Instead, take the time to figure out what's going to make you happy. Then, find a blueprint for that success that is uniquely your own, and emphasizes your strengths.

Finding the balance between "following good advice" and "discovering your own blueprint for success" can sometimes be tricky. That's because you'll often get tried-and-true tips from books (like this one), seminars, supervisors, or even mentors. But if the advice doesn't work for you, or doesn't fit with what you're trying to achieve, then you'll have to decide whether to amend your plan or find a different solution.

Of course, that shouldn't be taken as license for you to ignore all the advice you get, or to shrug off hard work just because it "doesn't seem like your way." There aren't any shortcuts to the top, and you shouldn't try to fool yourself into thinking that you can, or would want to, reinvent the wheel when it comes to managing your career.

The point is that there are principles and ideas you can count on, like the ones you found in earlier chapters, that will help you regardless of the challenge you're facing or the next step that's ahead of you. But figuring out how and when to apply them, and what you should be working toward, all depends on your own personal talents and preferences. No one else can live your life, and you're the only one who has to be satisfied with the way you spend your days. Find your own blueprint for success using the tools I've outlined and a little bit of trial and error. Over time, you'll develop a sense for whether you're moving closer to or farther away from the things that truly give you satisfaction.

Isn't that what this book, and your career, is really all about?

CONCLUSION

In the previous chapters I've shared with you nearly two dozen pieces of advice that have served me – and tens of thousands of other successful people – very well over the years. I hope you'll be able to take them and achieve your own dreams, whatever they may be.

As a last thought on the subject, let me remind you that finding success is hardly ever easy, but it's always worth it.

The biggest change you'll likely have to make will be in your own focus, attitude, and habits. The men and women who make it to the top do so intentionally. Success doesn't come to them accidentally — it's the result of a continuous effort that takes place over days, months, years, and sometimes even decades. They experience the same setbacks, course changes, and discouraging bad luck that the rest of us do. But they don't let anything dissuade them from their ultimate goal.

Remember as you move through your career that perseverance and tenacity are important qualities, and ones that you don't necessarily instill in yourself overnight. Having the desire to live a great life is one thing, but developing the strength to keep pushing through when times are tough and you're being tested is quite another.

Don't beat yourself up if you occasionally fail, make a bad decision, or find yourself going backward. It's happened to me and nearly everyone else I know at some point or another. Just keep reminding yourself of what you are trying to accomplish and take the best course of action you can find at the moment to keep getting closer.

Also, know that the world isn't necessarily going to cooperate with your plans. Competitors are going to get in the way, and events that are completely out of your control will occasionally seem to conspire against you. I've seen brilliant, hard-working people have to start from the bottom up, or undergo career changes, because a company or economy has collapsed. In each case, what seemed like a terrible ending point turned out to be a momentary speedbump, and an experience that caused them to learn and grow.

The ideas in this book aren't revolutionary, but they can be life-changing. What's more, many of them are never actually expressed or explained out loud, which is why so many men and women feel lost when it comes to moving their careers forward.

If you've made it this far, you now know what it takes to reach the top of your field and industry. You are ready to learn new things, work harder and smarter, become a leader, and understand how to get others to recognize your talents and help you grow in your field. That puts you at a distinct advantage when compared to most of the men and women you see going to work every morning. What you do with that advantage is entirely up to you.

It is my sincere hope that you're going to take the advice you have found and use it to do great things – for yourself, your company, and your industry. I'll be rooting for you, but creating success is a personal endeavor.

The choice is yours: Will you keep hoping for the life you want to come to you… or make a plan to go out and get it?

Carl Henry is a sales educator, keynote speaker and corporate consultant. During the course of his own successful career, he developed The MODERN Sales System, which he has been sharing with companies and associations around the world for many years.

A Certified Speaking Professional and a member of the National Speakers Association, Carl teaches essential sales skills with humor, insight and personal experience. Hundreds of companies throughout a diverse range of industries have used his highly-acclaimed seminars to educate and inspire their sales teams.

Carl's other books include The MODERN Sales System, The PEOPLE Approach to Customer Service and 15 Hot Tips that Will Supercharge Your Sales Career.

He currently lives in Charlotte, North Carolina.

To order additional copies of this book, or find out about Carl's seminars contact him at:

Henry Associates
704-847-7390
9430 Valley Road Charlotte, NC 28270
chenry@carlhenry.com
www.carlhenry.com

To order additional copies of this book contact:

Henry Associates
704-847-7390
9430 Valley Road Charlotte, NC 28270
chenry@carlhenry.com
www.carlhenry.com

www.ingramcontent.com/pod-product-compliance
Lightning Source LLC
Chambersburg PA
CBHW031948190326
41519CB00007B/714